Darkness Falls

A Double Bill

Jonathan Holloway and W. W. Jacobs

A SAMUEL FRENCH ACTING EDITION

SAMUEL FRENCH

FOUNDED 1830

SAMUELFRENCH-LONDON.CO.UK
SAMUELFRENCH.COM

ISBN 978-0-573-10002-4

www.samuelfrench-london.co.uk

www.samuelfrench.com

FOR AMATEUR PRODUCTION ENQUIRIES

UNITED KINGDOM AND WORLD
EXCLUDING NORTH AMERICA
plays@SamuelFrench-London.co.uk
020 7255 4302/01

Each title is subject to availability from Samuel French,

depending upon country of performance.

DARKNESS FALLS

This double bill was commissioned by The Palace Theatre Watford and received its first public performance on 29th January 1999, with the following cast:

The Monkey's Paw

Mother	Suzy Aitchison
Father	Philip Bretherton
Herbert White	Darren Tunstall
Sergeant-Major Morris	Angus Kennedy
Man From The Works	Angus Kennedy

The Dark

Simian Black	Philip Bretherton
Richard Legg	Darren Tunstall
Emma Landon-Philes	Suzy Aitchison
Tony Price	Angus Kennedy

Directed by Giles Croft
Designed by Neil Irish

AUTHOR'S NOTES

The Monkey's Paw

The play is divided into five scenes, each of which is separated by a passage of time. The scene breaks must be short, all the necessary props should be set prior to curtain up and only the actors in the play should move them. Once Herbert disappears from the action, he should not be seen again. The radio is an important presence, and during later scene breaks its ethereal static seems to provide mysterious echoes of distant lands and unquiet spirits.

While this adaptation stays faithful to the essential elements of W.W. Jacobs' classic short story, some liberties have been taken. Most notably the location is set resolutely in the industrial north of England, the date is now 1948 and the Whites' first son has played an active part in the history of the paw. Indeed, the largely invented character of Steven will play a surprising role in the evening's events.

Louis N. Parker's earlier stage adaptation has played no part in the decisions made during the writing of this play.

The Dark

Although the play is contemporary, it has a self-conscious old-fashioned style. This does not mean it should be treated as pastiche. The acting needs to be brisk, buoyant and the plot should be taken utterly seriously. For a useful reference watch the 1945 Ealing film *Dead of Night*.

Astute readers will note the set for **The Dark** shares most of the elements present in **The Monkey's Paw,** with the addition of a lateral partition wall half way US.

Jonathan Holloway

Other plays by Jonathan Holloway published
by Samuel French Ltd

Les Miserables
adapted from the novel by Victor Hugo

THE MONKEY'S PAW

CHARACTERS

Mother (Mrs White); early 40s
Father (Mr White); late 40s
Herbert White (Mr and Mrs White's son); early 20s
Sergeant-Major Morris; early 40s
Man From The Works; early 40s

SCENE: The combined kitchen and living-room of a modest working-class
Sunderland household

TIME — late 1940s

THE MONKEY'S PAW

Scene 1

The combined kitchen and living-room of a modest working-class Sunderland household. Evening

The house is in a row of terraced cottages situated up a hill in an isolated location a short distance from town. The Whites are owner-occupiers who feel disappointed that post-war depression has forced Father into unemployment, and nudged their once proud terrace into decline

There is a door R which opens on to a front path. DR *of the door is a window, through which foliage can be seen, and in front of which sits a sideboard. There is a row of coat pegs on the wall behind the door, with coats on them. The room is dominated by a coal-burning kitchen range* UC *with a comfortable upright chair by it. There are a kitchen table and chairs* DC. *Family treasures occupy a high mantelpiece, including a picture of the Whites' son Steven in uniform, a figure of the Madonna and a prized chess set. To the* L *of the range, on a low table, sits a large valve radio, with a dial that lights up when it is switched on. A staircase rises* L, *providing a natural divide between the main room and a scullery* L, *from which leads the back door to the yard. In the scullery there is a sink and a bracket with keys hanging from it*

When the play begins, rain and occasional gusts of wind can be heard from outside and the radio (illuminated) plays a Forties dance hit. The range is lit and glowing. Father and Herbert sit at the kitchen table absorbed in a game of chess. Mother bustles about in the background, preparing a meal of meat and vegetables. She jigs and hums along to the radio

Mother stops and listens to something outside. She turns the radio off, listens, then goes to the front door and opens it to look out. The room is invaded by wind and rain

Father Close it will you, please, Mother.
Herbert Please, Mother.
Mother (*closing the door*) The weather's filthy tonight. I'm worried he'll miss us. It's easy to get lost on the lane. Precious little light to see by.
Father Fought his way across Burma. I think he might manage.

Mother Listen to the wind.
Herbert I'm listening. Check.
Father Besides. He's three-quarters of an hour late. I doubt he's going to make an appearance tonight.
Herbert Mate.
Father That's the worst of living so far out. Of all the nasty, slushy, out-of-the-way places to live in, this is the worst. Path's a bog and the road's a torrent. I don't know what the Council are thinking about. I suppose because only two houses in the terrace are occupied, they think it doesn't matter.
Mother Don't get bad-tempered, love. Perhaps you'll win the next game.
Herbert That's the gate. He's here.
Mother Quick, Father. Get cleared away and open the door.

Father opens the door

Father Matthew. In you come, old friend.

Matthew Morris steps inside. His huge military-style waterproof sprays water everywhere. He wears a black leather glove on his left hand throughout

Morris I'm sorry, Jean. I've got water all over your floor. (*He clambers out of his coat*)
Mother (*moving to Matthew and watching him remove his coat*) Don't worry. Hang up your coat over there. (*She indicates the pegs*)
Father (*closing the door*) I'd best take it out back, Matthew. Jean's all right about it now, but I'll get it in the neck later for not sorting you out.

Father hangs Morris's coat in the scullery during the following

Mother Lovely to see you, Matthew. This is my son, Herbert.
Morris A pleasure, young man.
Herbert Likewise, sir.
Morris "Sir". Blimey! You've got him well-trained, Jean.
Mother So long as he's not being sarcastic.
Father He's never sarcastic, Jean.
Mother It's the fashion, these days. They're all sarcastic on the wireless. Now. Sit down by the fire, Matthew. What's the matter with your hand?
Morris Got it burned, Jean. Still works well enough. But it doesn't look too nice.
Father Fetch out the whisky for Matthew, will you Herbert.

Herbert gets a bottle of whisky and a glass from the sideboard during the following and pours a glass for Morris

Morris I'm not used to Matthew. Can't tell who you're talking about.
Sergeant-Major Morris, that's me. And I've been him for nearly twenty
years. Call me Morris, if you please.
Father Well then. Morris.
Morris That'll do just fine. (*To Herbert*) Ah, thanks, son. Drop of hot water
with that, please. Army style.

*Herbert pours some hot water from the kettle into the glass. Morris is settled
into the upright chair by the fire*

Mother It's good to see you again, Matthew ... Morris. Feels like only
yesterday we were playing about down the alley.
Morris Time rushes by, Jean.

Herbert gives Morris his whisky

Thanks, son. Make the best of it, Herbert. (*He looks at Herbert*) Heavens,
Jean. He certainly is the spit of his brother.

Mother and Father stop their activity for a moment

Mother Yes. He is. Sometimes I catch a sideways look at him, when I'm not
expecting to. And it's as if time had gone backwards, and it's Steven here
again.
Morris He was a good boy. I was glad to serve with him, Jean.
Mother (*emotional*) It was kind of you to sort things out for us. It's a terrible
thing to be so far away, and not able to make sure your child gets a decent
burial.
Father Well, that's the past, and this is now. And I'm just as proud of Herbert.
Morris Indeed. Glad to hear it.
Father Twenty-one years in the army. When you went away, you were just
a slip of a youth working in the warehouse. Now look at him, Jean.
Mother He doesn't look to have taken much harm.
Father Seems odd to be giving it up, Morris. The army's been good to you.
Morris Doubt there'll be another big war. Leastways, not one anybody's
going to walk away from. And the days of Empire ... That'll all be over and
done with soon. Well, got to face up to it. Best edge out before I get pushed.
Father The Empire, eh? I don't understand why those natives are so eager
to get rid of us. Only means returning to a time when life was cheap, and
corruption rife. Don't know when they're well off. Still, I'd like to go to
India myself, one day. Just to look around a bit, you know.
Morris Better off where you are. Beside this nice fire.
Father I should like to see those old temples and fakirs and jugglers.
Working in the yard, all through the war, feels like I missed out.

Morris I wouldn't complain. If I'd had a choice between working in the yard and seeing some of the things ... Well, I tell you, there's no contest in it.

Herbert But the colours and sights. I think you're so lucky to have seen all that.

Morris True, I suppose. And I don't want to make it seem as if I haven't got something out of it all. But, Herbert, you know, it's not just sitting around drinking char, and the like. I've had to do firing squads for the courts. I've even had to burn down hospitals because they were being used to shelter enemies of the Crown.

Mother Oh, dear. That sounds awful.

Herbert But what about magic?

Morris Ah.

Mother Nonsense, Herbert. What made you say that?

Herbert Father told me. You talked about it the other night, in the pub.

Mother I'll swear the two of you are as soft as each other. Father and son.

Herbert And Steven too. He was keen on mysteries. (*He turns to Morris*) He collected stuff about spirits and that. Mother threw it all out.

Mother You're going the right way to upset me, Herbert.

Morris Well, Jean. I came to believe some of it, right enough.

Mother Really, Morris? I wouldn't have thought ... You, of all people.

Morris It's not the sort of magic you imagine over here. Witches, and all that. It's more to do with the power of the mind. And religion. I don't know how to make sense of it myself, so I don't know why I'm going on.

Herbert Please, Mr Morris. Don't stop.

Morris It's like, if you can make somebody believe something, then it becomes real.

Mother I can believe I'll get rich. Guarantee it won't happen, though.

Morris That's because you don't really believe it. Right inside.

Father What will you do?

Morris Take a few months to look about. Then, maybe go south to see my old soldiering friends. Then, who knows? Australia, maybe.

Mother Why so far away?

Morris Nothing to keep me. Besides, I'm keen to put some distance between me and the past.

Father Secrets, Morris?

Morris No.

Herbert Dad was telling me about some spooky business. Something to do with India. What was it, Dad?

Father About a monkey's paw. You started telling me the other day about a monkey's paw. Like a rabbit's foot or something.

Morris Oh, that's nothing. (*He becomes shifty. During the following he displays reluctance to take the conversation in that direction, but allows himself to be coaxed. It should become evident that while Morris is* *"acting" a reluctance to talk about the paw, actually his manner is calculated to encourage the other men to dig deeper)* Leastways nothing worth hearing about.

Mother A monkey's paw? What, like a little dried-up hand?

Herbert That sounds pretty good. Like that film. *The Beast with Five Fingers.*

Morris Well, it's just a bit of what you might call magic, perhaps. (*He reaches into his pocket, takes out a monkey's paw and holds it for them to see*) To look at, it's just an ordinary little paw, dried to a mummy. (*He makes to put the paw away*)

Herbert (*indicating that he would like to examine the paw more closely*) Please. Can I have a proper look, Mr Morris?

Morris places the paw on the table

Father And what is there that's so special about it?

Morris This charm has had an unusual spell put on it. Anyhow, that's what they say. An old magician — a fakir — a very holy man; he wanted to show his village that fate rules people's lives, and those who interfere with fate do so to their sorrow.

Herbert How does it do that, Mr Morris?

Morris He put a spell so that three separate men could each have three wishes from it. Each of them has to own it — to have bought it — one from the next.

Father Sounds like a pretty good deal.

Morris Yes. I suppose it does.

Herbert Well, have you had your three, sir?

The family laugh awkwardly

Morris (*blanching*) I have.

Mother And did you have the three wishes granted?

Morris I did.

Mother And has anybody else wished?

Morris The first man had his three wishes. Yes. I don't know what the first two were, but the third was for death. That's how I got the paw.

Mother That's awful.

Herbert I don't see it. You said you have to have bought it. But if he was dead, how could you?

Morris I paid for his funeral.

Mother It'll be like the horoscopes in the newspaper. You wish for something, not expecting to get it. Then, if anything half-way like you asked for happens, you're convinced.

Morris No, Jean. That's not how it works. I said, I can't explain it. But you
get exactly what you asked for. Exactly. Only, the way it comes about —
that's what you don't expect.

Father If you've had your three wishes, it's no good to you now, then,
Morris. What do you keep it for?

Morris Fancy, I suppose. I did have some idea of selling it. But I don't think
I will. It has caused enough mischief already. Besides, people won't buy.
They think it's a fairy tale, some of them; and those who do think anything
of it want to try it first and pay me afterwards.

Mother Seems fair.

Morris It just won't work like that, Jean.

Father If you could have another three wishes, would you want them?

Morris I don't know. (*Suddenly very dark*) I don't know. (*He throws the paw
into the fire*)

Father snatches the paw out of the fire with a poker

Morris Best let it burn.

Father If you don't want it, Morris, sell it to me. (*He slams some coins on
the table*)

Morris I won't take that. I threw it on the fire. If you keep it, don't blame me
for what happens. Pitch it on the fire again like a sensible man.

Father How do you use it to make a wish?

Morris Hold it up in your right hand and wish aloud. But I warn you: there
will be consequences.

Mother Sounds like the Arabian Nights. Don't you think you might wish for
four pairs of hands for me.

*Father holds the paw up as if ready to make a wish. Morris lunges forward
and takes Father's wrist*

Morris If you must wish, then wish for something sensible.

Mother And let's all be sensible. Clear away, and let's sit up for supper.

Father I'll look after it, Morris. (*He drops the paw in his pocket*) Herbert,
fetch another whisky for us, please.

Mother I hope you're hungry, Morris.

Morris Famished, Jean.

The Lights dim

The radio comes on; the dial lights up and we hear a 1940s dance hit

SCENE 2

The same. Later the same evening

It is still raining. The table has been cleared. In the scullery, Herbert is drying the dishes as his mother washes them. Father is seated beside the range with a glass of whisky

The music fades and the radio light goes off

Mother I hope Morris catches his train. Terrible to be stranded on a night like this. He's got an odd manner these days. Not something I remember.

Herbert If the story about the monkey's paw is anything like those other tall tales of his, then we shan't make a fortune out of it.

Mother What took you so long at the gate with him, Father?

Herbert Did you talk him into taking the money?

Father Quite right, Herbert. Yes I did.

Herbert Really? You got it off him, Father?

Mother (*after a silence*) They've got a word for you on the radio. Sucker.

Father A few shillings, that's all. A token, you'd call it. He didn't want it, but I made him take it. And he told me all over again to throw the trinket away.

Herbert I don't completely believe it. But then, I suppose I want to believe it. So ...

Mother I don't think Father David would approve of us talking this way.

Herbert Just another sort of magic.

Mother reacts badly to this

Father Herbert. Please.

Herbert Sorry. Anyway, like as not we're going to be rich, and famous, and happy. Come on, Father. Wish to be an emperor, straight off. Then you can't be henpecked.

Mother That's exactly what I mean, Herbert. Cheekiness and sarcasm.

Father (*taking the paw from his pocket and looking at it*) I don't know what to wish for, and that's a fact.

There is a sudden, awkward stillness in the room. Father looks up at the other two

Oh, don't worry. You two are safe enough. It seems to me I have all I want.

Mother and Herbert relax, but it is clear they do not wholly believe Father

Herbert If you could clear the mortgage on the house, you and Mother would be quite happy, wouldn't you? Well, wish for four hundred pounds, then.

That will just do it. (*He grabs two wooden spoons and does a drum roll on a saucepan*)
Father (*holding up the paw*) I wish for four hundred pounds.

Herbert strikes a pan lid as though it is a cymbal. His father screams and drops the paw

Father It moved. As I said the wish. It twisted in my hand like a snake.
Herbert Well, I don't see the money. (*He picks up the paw and puts it back on the table*) And I bet I never shall.
Mother It must have been your imagination, Father.
Father Never mind, though. There's no harm done. But it gave me a shock all the same.

They all settle down at the table. The wind rises outside. A door bangs upstairs. They all start

Mother What was that?
Father Perhaps I should have a look around upstairs.

Herbert ascends the stairs with exaggerated trepidation. Mother is taken in by his acting. Herbert peers on to the landing, and seems startled

Herbert I know exactly what it was.
Mother What?
Herbert Boris Karloff knocking over the towel stand.
Mother There. Sarcasm!
Herbert (*turning on the stairs and descending as Bela Lugosi; speaking with a ludicrous Lugosi accent*) I expect you'll find the cash tied up in a big bag in the middle of your bed. And something horrible squatting up on top of the wardrobe watching you as you pocket your ill-gotten gains.
Mother I'm off to bed. (*She bustles towards the stairs, then stops, suddenly nervous*) Coming up, Father?
Father Yes.

Father and Mother ascend the stairs and exit

Herbert hangs back

Herbert Good-night. (*He sits at the table, eager to finish his dad's whisky. He drains the glass*)
Mother (*calling, off*) Herbert! You've got work in the morning.

Herbert puts the glass down and accidentally brushes the paw, startling himself

The Lights dim. The radio light comes on and the radio plays an early recording of Frank Sinatra singing "Blue Skies"

SCENE 3

The same. The following morning

A bright morning scene; the storm has passed. The music fades and the radio light goes out

Herbert sits at the table, finishing a hearty breakfast. He notices the paw at the edge of the table, and moves it to the sideboard. During the following he gets himself ready for work

Mother enters

Mother I suppose all old soldiers are the same. And we sat there listening to his nonsense. How could magic wishes be granted in these modern days?

Father enters

And if they could, how would four hundred pounds hurt you, Father?

Herbert Might drop right out of the sky, and bang him on the head.

Father Funny, when he talked about it last week, he said the things happened so naturally that you could explain them away as coincidence. Then last night he said something different: that you get exactly what you asked for. Why'd he contradict himself?

Mother Because it's all so much baloney, that's why. "A fool and his money." Still, we'll have to consider what you paid as our ticket price for the entertainment.

Herbert Well, don't start spending your new fortune before I get home from work. I'm afraid it will turn you into a mean, avaricious man, and we shall have to disown you.

Father I don't think you need worry on that account. Sudden riches don't come to the likes of us. We're made to just get on with it. If you can keep your job, and put food on the table ——

Mother And find a nice lass.

Father And find a nice lass. Yes. That's about the best we've got to look forward to.

Mother bundles Herbert into his overcoat

Herbert Talking of lasses, I was thinking of inviting Harriet Blunstone over
   for tea next Saturday.
Mother Don't you dare. I don't want you getting mixed up with that family.
Herbert (*throwing his head back and laughing*) Yer all right, Mother. I
   don't even speak to her. It was just to get you going.

*Mother bundles Herbert out of the door, and waves him off with great
affection*

   (*Off*) Bye, then.
Mother Bye.
Father (*distracted for a moment*) And another thing. That throwing it on the
   fire business. He told me it couldn't be burnt up. "Impervious to flame",
   he said. Until the third owner finished with it.
Mother That's the postman, Father. It looks like he's got something for us.
Father Really? I wasn't expecting a letter.
Mother Oh, dear. You don't think it's something bad?

   Father exits through the front door

*The following exchange comes from off stage, as if it is occurring up the
garden path*

Father (*off*) Have you got something for me today?
Postman (*off*) Ay, just the one.
Father (*off*) Thanks very much.

   Father enters carrying a brown envelope

Mother Looks like a bill.
Father Or a cheque from the football pools. (*He opens the envelope and
   reads*) No. It's a bill. Second payment on that suit I got made up in the
   summer.
Mother Good job Herbert wasn't here. He'd have made some more of his
   funny remarks. Seeing the way we looked at that envelope. (*She turns the
   radio on, and goes about her work*)

Father makes up the fire

*The Lights dim. The volume comes up on the radio. We hear short wave static,
with the strange undulating whines of tuning to distant lands. The volume
drops again to silence and the light fades*

SCENE 4

The same. Later

Father is standing at the window, looking out, thinking

Mother is now wearing a housecoat. She places a plate of sandwiches on the table

Mother Stop brooding, Father. There's something for your dinner.
Father Brooding. I dare say. But for all that. That thing moved in my hand. I'll swear to it.
Mother You thought it did.
Father I say it did. There was no "thought" about it. I had just ...
Mother What's the matter?
Father There's a fellow. Hanging about at the gate. Looks like he wants something. Back in a jiffy.

Father opens the front door and walks off down the path

Mother goes to the window and watches the men. She realizes they are coming inside and makes a frantic effort to tidy the table and herself during the following

Father enters alone

Father Jean. It's a fellow from the works.
Mother What does he want?
Father (*ignoring Mother; speaking to the man outside*) Will you step this way, sir?
Mother (*in an exaggerated stage whisper*) Heavens! No, Father. (*She wrenches her housecoat off and hangs it up*) Wait just a moment, will you? (*She stands back quickly, tidying herself*)

The Man enters and remains silent, fingering his hat in his hands

Father goes to stand beside Mother. The couple stare at the man

Father Well now, how can we help you, sir?

No reply

(*Trying a different tack*) It's a way up the hill, all right.

Man That's true. Quite a climb.

Father Will you sit down, maybe?

Man No. I'm sorry to disturb your day. Like I said — outside — I was asked to call, you see.

Mother Who by?

Man I work at Maw and Meggins.

Mother Yes.

Man In the wages office.

Mother (*her face fixed in a frightened smile*) Is anything the matter?

Man Yes. I'm afraid there is.

Father Is there some trouble?

Man No.

Mother Has something happened to Herbert? What is it? What's the matter with him?

Father There, there, Mother. Sit down and don't jump to conclusions. He's not brought bad news, I'm sure.

Man I'm sorry. I'm afraid that I have.

Mother Is he hurt?

Man He's not in any pain. No, not at all.

Mother Oh, thank God! Thank God for that! We should come down, shouldn't we? (*She rises*) I'll get my coat, shall I? No. Father. You fetch the coats. I'll pour this fellow a cup of tea. You'll take a cup, won't you? There's one in the pot. I just made it for ... (*She weakly indicates the sandwiches on the table*) I mean, to have with ... Thank ——

Man (*cutting her off*) No! (*Conscious he has been too forceful*) There's no point. No doubt the police will be up soon.

Mother What? Why would they?

Man (*very deliberately*) He was caught in the machinery.

Father Caught in the machinery. Yes.

The couple hold hands very tightly

Father He's the only one left to us. Our other boy ...

Man I'm so sorry.

Father I can't believe it. He was laughing fit to bust as he went out. This is too hard, sir.

Man (*moving to the window and staring out*) The firm wished me to convey to you their sincere sympathy for you in your great loss. Please, I beg that you understand I am only their servant and merely obeying orders. Now then. They wish to say that Maw and Meggins disclaim all responsibility. They will admit no liability at all. But in consideration of your son's services — and, indeed, your own, when you were with the firm, for that matter — they wish to present you with a certain sum as compensation. There has to be nothing further, though. No issue of court proceedings and the like, if you understand.

The couple release each other's hands, and turn to look at the Man

Father How much have you brought us?
Man This envelope contains a cash sum of four hundred pounds.

Mother sobs; she stays on stage through the following scene change

Father and the Man exit

The Lights dim. The radio light comes on: the BBC has closed down, and we hear the distant chatter of exotic languages buried behind the faint hiss of static

SCENE 5

The same. Night

An oil lamp is set in the centre of the table

The Lights come up on a night-time setting; the oil-lamp illuminates Mother's stricken face. The sound of the radio fades out and the light goes off

Father comes downstairs in his dressing-gown, looking for Mother

Mother How Morris must have hated us.
Father What do you mean?
Mother To have come here. To have found us out after all these years. Just to do this to us.
Father Come to bed, Moth ... Jean. It's cold now the fire's gone out.
Mother It is colder for my son. Herbert. My dearest Herbert. (*She bows her head and weeps into the table-top*)

Father moves to the table. He sits. Mother stops crying and looks up at Father

Mother Haven't you worked it out yet?
Father What, Jean?
Mother Morris being with our Steven when he died. Sorting out the funeral. The paw's first owner. It was Steven, wasn't it? What in Heaven's name happened to make Morris hate us so? No, not "Heaven's name".
Father That's just imagination, Jean. Come to bed.
Mother You know what we must do.
Father No, Jean. I don't want to talk about it. Please. Let's not go over it again, and again.

Mother It doesn't have to be a curse. We were unwise, that's all.

Father I don't believe there was any connection. We talked about coincidence. That's all it was.

Mother You said it moved in your hand. You believed it then. And Morris talked about fate — and what he called the consequences of changing things around.

Father Please don't go on with this.

Mother Where is it?

Father Look. It doesn't matter.

Mother I want it. You haven't destroyed it, have you?

Father I wish I could. I wish I'd never touched it, let it alone before I could be so stupid.

Mother There! You do believe in it.

Mother searches the drawers and clears shelves, sending mantelpiece treasures flying. She is oblivious to the damage she is doing

Where have you put the monkey's paw?

Father It's hanging up with the keys. In the scullery. On the bracket.

Mother (*suddenly laughing with disturbing glee*) The other two wishes. We've only had one.

Father (*aghast*) Wasn't that enough!

Mother No. We'll have one more. Go and get it. Quickly! Herbert's in the wet and the cold. Get it. Get it!

Father If we do this, will you stop? Will you let it rest? (*He fetches the paw from the scullery during the following*)

Mother I can't do it. You're the owner. You will have to do it.

Father What do you want me to say?

Mother It's simple. Wish our boy alive again.

Father Good God! What have we turned into? We're both mad.

Mother Wish it true. Oh, my boy. My son.

Father Please, Jean. Let's go back to bed. You don't know what you're saying.

Mother We had the first wish granted. Why not the second?

Father Coincidence. I said ——

Mother He said it might look like coincidence. Might. Look. He wasn't telling the truth. He wanted rid of it because he was too stupid to use it wisely. Australia! No wonder! (*Terrifyingly*) Wish it, damn you!

Father Jean. He's been dead ten days. And besides ... I couldn't tell you, but — I was only able to recognize him by his clothing. All down one side ... His face, and his arm ... Look, Jean. If he was too terrible for you to see then, think of what ten days in the earth will have done ...

Mother Bring him back. Do you think I fear the child I nursed? Wish it!

Father This is foolish. And it's wicked to want such a thing, Jean. Please.

Mother Wish!

Father (*raising the paw*) I wish my son alive again. (*He lets the paw fall to the floor, then slumps into a chair*)

Mother watches from the window, staring transfixed into the night

There is a long pause. Nothing happens

Mother lets the curtain fall back across the window, and, seemingly weakened, sits beside her husband. Their hands find one another on the table-top, and they sit still and united

There is a quiet scratching at the door. A pause. Then another scratching sound

Father hears the noise and moves quietly to the door

Mother What's that?

Father pushes the top bolt home, then turns and places his back against the door

Father A rat. It's a rat. I saw it in the yard last night.

A huge knock resounds through the house

Mother Herbert. My son. He's come back. It's Herbert! (*She runs to the door*)

Father (*barring the way*) What are you going to do?

Mother It's my boy. It's Herbert. I forgot the cemetery is a mile away. He needed time. What are you stopping me for? Let go. I must open the door.

Father For God's sake, don't let it in.

Mother You're afraid of your own son? Let me go. I'm here. Herbert. It's me.

There is another knock at the front door, then more knocking, continuing under the following

Mother strains to reach to the topmost bolt; Father restrains her and the couple struggle viciously

Mother The bolt. Help me. I can't reach it.

Father pushes Mother off and lunges for the monkey's paw

Mother recovers herself, dashes for the bolt and draws it back

Father (*holding the paw aloft*) I wish my son Herbert at peace with God. (*He slowly opens his palm, held high as if giving a blessing. It is empty*)

The knocking stops. Mother hauls open the door

A cold breeze invades the room. Moonlight is seen beyond the doorway. But no-one is there

There is a long moment of suspense, then Mother's shoulders slump. She closes the door very slowly, turns, and moves towards the stairs. She sees Steven's photo, picks it out of the debris and places it carefully on the table. She begins climbing the stairs

There is another knock, from the back door this time. The couple are stunned to hear the sound, and stare towards it

Father (*the truth dawning*) It does things a crooked way.

Again the heavy, urgent knocking

(*Looking at the photo on the table*) We had two sons, Jean. Oh, merciful Heavens. Two.
Mother Steven. (*She smiles*)
Father Oh, God help us. God in Heaven, help us please.

The sound of knocking — now with an echo effect — becomes unbearably loud, filling the auditorium

THE CURTAIN DROPS QUICKLY

THE DARK

CHARACTERS

Simian Black: ex-Cambridge don, 40s
Richard Legg: novelist, born in the North East, 30s
Emma Landon-Philes: a successful actress, 30s
Tony Price: a journalist, 30s

SCENE: The living-room of a substantial eighteenth century house on the Northumberland coast

TIME: the present

THE DARK

The living-room of a substantial eighteenth century house on the Northumberland coast. The present day. The night of New Year's Eve

The living-room is elegant. Double doors c open on to a hallway, with the front door out of view off R. A staircase can be half seen rising from the hall towards L. From the living-room, another door leads off L to the dining-room. There is a cocktail cabinet R on which a selection of malt whiskies is arranged alongside a large valve radio, the dial of which lights up when it is switched on. A tastefully decorated Christmas tree stands beside the cabinet. There is an elegant French period style armchair R, and the centre of the room is dominated by an expensive sofa, in front of which sits an elegant coffee table with an ashtray and table lighter. A small occasional table L of the sofa carries a telephone, address book and table lamp. There is a fireplace with a high mantelpiece DL. A clock and cigar box share the mantel

When the play begins, the room is deserted, illuminated by a single table lamp. There is a cosy fire in the grate. A gale is blowing outside. The Christmas tree is illuminated. The radio on the sideboard is tuned to Radio 4; an orchestra plays the closing phrases of Iolanthe

Radio Announcer (*with an easy manner, as if filling in time*) Before the nine o'clock news there's just time to tell you about this evening's late play. *The Monkey's Paw* is a seasonal tale of mystery and imagination, set in an isolated country house in the North East. Our cast includes Emma Landon-Philes, whose performance as Desdemona in *Othello* has won universal acclaim at London's Old Vic theatre. Tomorrow night, Tom Norrish will conduct the first in-depth interview with this remarkable young actress. So, we're privileged to be in her company tonight, at ten-thirty, cosied under the blankets with *The Monkey's Paw*.

There is a robust knock at the front door

Simian Black enters from the kitchen, carrying his jacket and sorting out his cuffs. He puts on his jacket and tidies himself ready to meet guests

There is another loud rapping at the door

Simian switches the lights on and tidies a cushion, making sure the room is just so

Another knock

Simian finally heads off into the hallway. He switches on the light in the hall and opens the unseen front door

The two men speak offstage, talking over the radio. (The director may use as much or as little of the next portion of radio speech as is needed)

The time is almost nine o'clock, and this is the BBC. Just before we go to the newsroom, we have a message that the Meteorological Office has issued a warning of severe weather in the North East and Borders areas. Strong winds and sleet, turning to snow, are expected in the North Eastern region. (*Pause*) And I see from the clock that we've just enough time to tell you more about our programmes for the holiday period. Tomorrow afternoon we begin a new classic serial, *The Lifted Veil*, based on the novella by George Eliot. This strange and uncharacteristic work reveals a darker side to the author of *The Mill on the Floss*. Shaken by the death of her sister, Eliot became transfixed by the occult, and was consumed by a passion to lift the veil of death and make contact with the other side. Eliot's unlikely hero, Latimer, is cursed with second sight, including the ability to read the minds of others and to foresee the exact date and time of his own death. This compelling tale ranges across the capitals of

Simian (*off*) Good-evening, Richard. I'm Simian. I'm glad you could make it. But you're the first to arrive, I'm afraid.

Richard (*off*) Isn't Emma here? Bloody hell! She was supposed to be coming up earlier on.

Simian (*off*) No. You're definitely the first. Unless she's hiding. Please do come in. It's filthy out there, isn't it? That's the worst of living so far out. Of all the nasty, slushy, out-of-the-way places to live in, this is the worst. Path's a bog and the road's a torrent. I don't know what the Council are up to. I suppose because there's only one house on the road, they think it doesn't matter. Are you very wet?

Richard (*off*) Yes, I am. Sorry about your floor. What can I do with my coat?

Simian (*off*) Oh, that's all right. We'll hang it here.

Europe, conjuring a mysterious world of miraculous visions, poisoning, desire, damnation and ultimate liberation on the windswept Alps. And, by way of contrast, New Year's Day marks the beginning of our new season of live comedy shows recorded at last year's Edinburgh Festival. "Whoops there goes my Sporran" brings new Scots comedy talent to the airwaves ...

Simian and Richard enter. Richard has a small cut on his cheek

It doesn't matter. Do get into the warm. I'm sorry about the radio. (*He turns the radio off*) I keep it on all the time. Company.

Richard (*slumping on to the sofa*) Bloody difficult place to find. I thought I must have got it wrong. Couldn't see any lights from the road.

Simian Yes. I was in the kitchen. It's in the old part of the house. Right down the back. Forget people might need a beacon. Not very seasonal, I'm afraid. (*Suddenly dark*) Look, would you mind not swearing so much?

Richard (*startled*) Pardon? Sorry.

Simian (*returning to the cabinet to pour drinks. Friendly again*) Now. Can I offer you a drink?

Richard Yes. Have you got a beer?

Simian No. But I do have a couple of excellent malts. Islay or Speyside. Just right for a night like this.

Richard OK, then. Fine.

Simian Any preference? (*He indicates two different bottles*)

Richard No. Wouldn't know the difference.

Simian Right. (*He pours the drinks*) Here you are. (*He hands Richard a drink*) Try that.

Richard (*taking a sip and identifying the whisky*) Laphroaig.

Simian (*Touché! Smiling*) Very good. (*Pause*) I heard Emma mentioned on the radio. Shame you missed it.

Richard Don't worry, I hear quite enough about Emma. She's — all over the place.

Simian You don't sound too pleased.

Richard (*sighing*) No, of course I'm very pleased. She's an excellent actress. (*He pauses awkwardly. Then, with irony*) I guess I should thank you for this evening. I mean, I know these annual get-togethers are important to you all, and I'm sure it's a real honour to be invited along.

There is a pause. They both drink

Simian Nice of you to make the effort. We started up while I was still teaching. But our days are numbered. No fresh blood, so to speak. How did you meet Emma?

Richard That Midsummer Madness thing. Berkeley Square. Last summer. *(He slyly enjoys the chance of a good swear)* Stuck up twats and twatesses. Smeary, pissed-up pink faces all over the *Evening Standard*. My agent insisted I go. You can't avoid that kind of crap these days.

Simian It sounds glamorous to me.

Richard If you want to work in books, there's a lot of stuff like that. All these prizes. Can't avoid them. But you don't need to worry about a career now, do you?

Simian Inheriting this lot released me. I look back on teaching at Cambridge, and it feels like another life.

Richard You made a big impact on your students. Emma says you were the most important thing in their lives.

Simian You don't approve.

There is a pause. Richard shrugs

I'm sure some people at Cambridge thought the whole thing was unhealthy too. Saw me as a latter day Svengali.

Richard Impressive. The way they've stuck with you. I can't imagine wanting to keep in touch with my teachers.

Simian I hope it's because they like me. *(Pause)* But I'm a realist, and I know you can get away with a lot in a university. Impress young people in a way that just wouldn't wash anywhere else. You must have your own circle?

Richard No, I try to keep out of it all. "I don't belong to any set. I am not a member of any club."

Simian Samuel Butler.

Richard Yes, it is. Paraphrased anyway. I'm reading him again.

Simian Last thing he said was "Where's my cheque book?" When Butler was cremated, one bone reputedly survived the furnace. Butler's "friend" — another confirmed bachelor by the name of Henry Festing-Jones — is said to have kept it in a box on his mantelpiece, near Guildford. There's something pleasantly odd about that. Quite tickles me.

There is a pause; they drink. Richard's eye is drawn to the cigar box on the mantelpiece

But Emma and you. Six months on. Any plans?

Richard You'll have to ask her.

Simian Of course, you're doing very well too. Emma mentioned a film — er — on the telephone.

Richard I heard yesterday. *Black Heart* has been bought by an American company.

Simian Excellent. Well done!

Richard Emma's name was on the cast. Some Hollywood agent has been sniffing around her. Like a dog returning to yesterday's faeces.

Simian Charming turn of phrase.

Richard Well, I am a writer. (*He drinks*) Yeah, so her name obviously helped. Looks like it might be in production by this autumn.

Simian You must be excited?

Richard Frantic with it. It's just ... Oh, well — I wouldn't want posterity to remember me for *Black Heart*.

Simian You shouldn't do yourself down, or your audience. Your paperbacks are selling very well. It's an extraordinary achievement for anyone to make a decent living writing these days. Just think how awful it would have been if you'd drowned, or somesuch. Without ever having achieved anything.

Richard What made you say that?

Simian What?

Richard About drowning?

Simian Are you all right?

Richard School journey accident. When I was a kid. We were canoeing, and the bloke with me drowned

Simian I'm sorry. I didn't know. Maybe somebody was watching over you. (*He pauses*) You know, you should sit up straight. Gives a better impression.

Richard (*sighing but complying*) Still, my stuff is hardly great literature, is it? I had hoped to do something more profound. But if it's going to be airport books, I suppose I should make the best of it. I'm on the third Dark Angel novel at the moment, and it's much more difficult than the others were. Seem to have run out of road.

Simian Emma mentioned you were having trouble with it. Perhaps we'll have a chance to try some ideas. Mind you, if Warner Brothers end up wanting to film it, I'll expect a fee.

Richard Oh, don't worry. I never steal without at least printing a "dedication". I make it nine-fifteen. I thought everyone had to be here by nine-thirty for the toast. Where the fuck ... Sorry.

There is a loud knock at the door

Simian (*getting up*) Dead on cue. Help yourself to another drink, please.

Simian exits into the hall to answer the door

Richard gets up and goes to the sideboard

We hear the front door open

Simian (*off; animated*) Tony!
Tony (*off*) Hallo, Simian. Terrible journey.
Simian (*off*) How are you? I was getting worried.
Tony (*off*) I couldn't get away. Ended up running the newsroom.

Tony enters the room

Hallo there!

There is a moment of awkwardness

Simian Tony. Let me introduce you. Richard Legg —Tony Price. Richard
   is Emma's new boyfriend.
Richard Not so new, actually.
Simian Well, new since this time last year.
Tony I'm very pleased to meet you, Richard. Anyone who can get past
   Emma's defences deserves ... Well, I don't know what he deserves.
   Where's everybody else?
Simian Bad news. We're it.
Tony No. Oh, dear.
Simian Emma telephoned this afternoon. She'll be here.
Tony So, what about the others, Simian? Tim and Clara? And Gerald?
Simian They've gone "the way of all flesh". Wives, babies, "Aged Ps". A
   conspiracy of time and genealogy that leaves us high and dry.
Tony Everybody seems to have done so well. Hardly surprising they'd lose
   interest. Never mind.
Simian I do mind, actually. Very much as it happens. Drink, Tony?
Tony Yep. I'll take the cooking whisky in the cupboard.

*From here on the conversation is accompanied by serious drinking. The
characters take turns pouring drinks for one another, and at least a whole
bottle is consumed by the end of the scene*

Simian Still, we do have Richard's first visit to give us a sense of occasion.
   We'll put you centre stage next year, Tony.
Tony What? I don't understand what you're talking about half the time,
   Simian. (*He turns to Richard*) Richard. How did you find getting here?
Richard I drove. Separately from Emma. Had some trouble with the car.
   Took a tumble.
Simian Went into a ditch.

Richard Did I? Yes. I went into a ditch. Got a knock on the head. Still feel a bit odd, actually. I guess the car must be in a garage by now.

Simian Which garage?

Richard (*puzzling*) Oh — er — I'm not sure.

Tony Brave of you, dispatching it to God-knows-where. How did you get here?

Richard Um, the garage, I guess. Gave me a lift — I think ... Don't feel right, actually. Maybe I should stay off the drink.

Simian Don't worry. It has to be one of only three garages I can think of. We'll phone around tomorrow. Track the car down for you.

Richard What about you?

Tony I was suddenly stuck with the graveyard shift. Bloody Hogmanay's such a big deal now, no self-respecting Scot wants to be trapped in the office. "Give it to the English bugger!" But then someone threw himself off the castle esplanade. Gutted on the railings. Haggis all over the pavement. Course, suddenly I was far too junior to handle such a major event. So they called in an authentic Caledonian hack. I jumped in the car. Only took ten minutes to get out of Edinburgh. But blowing a gale. Horizontal sleet. Around eight, just level with Holy Island, disaster. Some poor sod in a sports car had crossed over the central reservation and gone right under a lorry. Bedlam. Traffic blocked for miles. Police. Firemen. Everything. Horrible. Couldn't help peering at the wreck. There'd been a fire. Totally burnt out. Disgusting.

Simian Oh, dear. That's someone's New Year off to a bad start.

Richard Funny way of putting it.

Simian Why?

Richard Well, the driver must have been killed.

Tony Yep. I guess so. I couldn't see properly. But I expect he was killed. (*He pauses*) Richard. I do believe there's a little cut. There, on your cheek.

Richard dabs his finger on the cut. He takes out his handkerchief and wipes his cheek

Richard Must have happened in the car.

Tony If this was a whodunit, that would be conclusive proof.

Richard What of?

Tony That you'd strangled some woman and she tried to rip your face off with her nails while you were doing it.

Simian Perhaps I should get some antiseptic?

Richard No. Really, I'm fine. You work in Edinburgh, then, Tony?

Tony The *Caledonian Times*.

Richard Great.

Tony Simian doesn't think so. Says I've wasted my talent. Calls it a provincial rag. You don't approve, do you, Simian?

Simian I'm saying nothing.

Tony My father thinks I should have been a doctor. Women's insides. That's where the money is, eh?

Simian Plenty of time for you to make your mark, Tony.

Richard Emma said you and she did plays together at Cambridge.

Tony Yes we did. I'm a pretty rancid journalist. But I would have made a truly terrible actor. Now then. Come on, what do you do, Richard?

Simian Richard's an author.

Tony Really. Excellent. What sort of thing do you write?

Richard I've got a series out. About a sort of supernatural detective. He's called The Dark Angel. He solves cases by using both his intelligence, and magic.

Tony What? Real magic? Black magic?

Richard It's got more intellectual plush than that. No. He's travelled in the East and applies a mixture of spiritual disciplines — some actual stuff, and some I just made up. There are two books so far. And I'm working on a third at the moment. Pretty difficult, actually. I've ground to a halt. You see, this detective, I haven't made up my mind how benign or malevolent he should be.

Simian He's both, of course. Everyone is.

Tony Excellent, Richard. I must read them. When we were at Cambridge everybody wanted to be an author. Or a real artist of some kind. Hardly anyone had the stamina to see it through, though. Still, there are a few who have gone on to do something half-way decent. Like Emma. (*He pauses as he stares into his drink*) Oh, and I mentioned Gerald earlier. Gerald O'Connor got to Cambridge entirely through his own efforts, and against the will of his dreadful father. The old fella drove Gerald up to college one time. Awful red-faced loon crammed behind the wheel of a clapped-out Maestro. Personally, I'd have made him park well away from the college. Old bugger hated culture on sight. Even so, Gerald took up painting. Can you believe it? In this day and age. Nothing to do with his studies, of course. Even so, he's made a good fist of it. Simian encouraged him. Simian, what's up with Gerald? How come he isn't here?

Simian Sorry, Tony. I was going to tell you later.

Tony Tell me? What?

Simian I'm afraid Gerald won't be coming. He's ... Well, he's not with us anymore.

Tony What do you mean?

Simian He's dead, Tony.

Tony No. Surely? You're joking, Simian.

Simian Afraid not.

Tony God! How did it happen?

Simian Suicide.

Tony Poor Gerald. Any idea why?

Simian No. Shut himself in a garage with the engine running.

Tony Christ! Things seemed to be coming together for him.

Simian Yes, that certainly appeared to be the case from the outside. But he used to get terribly depressed.

Tony Mmm. Well, it's true I got the impression there was some big secret lurking in the background. Tried to get it out of him once — when he was drunk. Joshua's wedding, last summer. Joshua Oliphant-Hope. Complete prat, Richard. Anyway, kept phoning old Gerald, and we managed a brief session in London in October. He'd started going to Church. And I saw one of his recent pictures! Morbid, mind you.

Simian What do you mean?

Tony He'd done this mad triptych thing. Three pictures of some chap who looked like Enoch Powell. But painted in the style of that goggle-eyed fellow who does those bent-up Popes.

Simian Contorted?

Tony That's right.

Simian Bacon.

Tony Yes. And these chaps have their guts hanging out.

Simian Like your Scotsman.

Tony Not the sort of thing you'd want over the fireplace. Used to do these lovely pictures of the Cam in summer. Funny what happens to artists when they grow up. The fun goes out of it, don't you think? It all gets murky, and stops making sense.

Simian I was worried last year. Looking back, seems like he'd almost made his mind up to give up the ghost.

Tony I had no idea he was so bad. Does Emma know about Gerald's death?

Simian Yes, she does.

Tony The two of them were very close, Richard. Went out together in their second year. Don't think he ever really got over her. Of course, that was all before he met up with Dorothy.

Richard Poor old Gerald.

Tony What?

Richard Nothing.

Simian Guess Gerald must have been more anxious about things than anybody could tell. A waste. (*He pauses*) Still, got to get on, eh? Please, Tony. Try and cheer up. Why don't we change the subject? Richard. What's this problem you're having with the book?

Richard I know what it's about, and I know what happens at the beginning, and how it ends. Problem is, tying the whole thing together. The driver has killed himself in order to defend the woman he loves — from a demon.

Tony Pardon?

Richard Mephistopheles. He's not a "devil-with-horns" sort of thing. My Mephistopheles wears a grey overcoat, a Homburg, speaks with a nasal whine — probably uses a Vick inhaler — and lives on the outskirts of suburban North London. Watford, somewhere like that. A sort of unsavoury bank clerk. The story starts ages ago at this time of year. The main character — he ends up as quite a successful writer — is still a student, and he's on his way home from a solitary West End drinking binge, on top of the night bus. It's New Year and he's staying with his parents — home from college and spending a lonely Christmas vacation. He walks, thinks, rides buses, drinks. He burns with loneliness and ambition. There is only one other man on board the bus. Our friend ——

Simian Mephistopheles.

Richard That's right, Simian. Our young man gets off the bus. It's very cold, and snow is falling. It swirls in illuminated cones of sodium yellow — under each street light. He turns down an alley way. His shoes mark the virgin snow. Behind him, another pair of shoes make a second, silent trail. The alley is long and broad — and terribly, terribly empty. Half-way along, and neither end is visible through the snow. A timeless, suspended, magical place. Our man leans back against a lamp-post, and turns his face upward to bask in the sodium glare, and to let the maelstrom of flakes sting his eyes. And he utters a vow — one which he believes, totally. He swears he will do anything to achieve his ambition — to be a writer.

Tony (*mischievously*) Hah! It could be you, Richard.

Richard Well, actually it was me. A bad time. Before my parents died. It all got a lot better after that. Anyway, back to the alley. So he gathers his coat around himself, and lurches onward, but immediately crashes into a man — grey coat and Homburg — who he had not seen approach. There is an oof! And a mumbled apology — and they part. The deal is done. The soul is signed away.

Tony But it can't be.

Richard Why?

Tony Surely, the damned man has to know he made the contract.

Simian No. So long as he knows he's made a commitment to ambition, whatever the cost.

Richard Yes. Good. He decides to be absolutely focused on realizing his ambitions: the rest — family, friends, relationships — it can all go to the devil! Anyway. Moving on. I want to connect the writer killing himself with Mephistopheles calling in the debt.

Simian Well, what about passion? Or ownership mistaken for passion. The writer ... Let's call him — what?

Richard Ashley.

Simian Ashley comes from humble origins, but is now extremely successful, and overly proud of it, and he's fallen for a young woman who comes from a privileged background. Ashley feels inferior, and gets obsessive about owning, dominating her. What's her name?

Richard Claire. The character's name is Claire.

Simian Claire doesn't fancy the idea of being in his shadow. She feels cornered. This coincides with Mephistopheles calling-in the hitherto unknown debt. Mephistopheles tempts Ashley with a chance to extend the time allowed him on earth, and to give him a re-vamped Claire, a compliant Claire, if Ashley can deliver her soul when the time is right. Ashley struggles to resist this temptation, but doesn't trust himself not to give in, and as a last defiant gesture against evil, kills himself, thus saving her from the demon's clutches. The story could end with Mephistopheles stalking the girl — and we'd feel damned frustrated that Ashley's sacrifice was in vain.

Tony Blimey! Sounds pretty good. I'd buy it. (*He pours fresh drinks during the following*) Except I know the story now. So, there wouldn't be much point.

Richard Very good, Simian. Thanks. By the way, I hope you won't mind, but I have made some changes to the character of the Dark Angel, based on what Emma told me about you. You've turned into a sort of model for him.

Simian Make sure you work from what you know. When writers are at their best, it's all coming straight from inside. It's all you, Richard. Like it or not — it's all up there. (*He indicates Richard's forehead*)

Richard There's a set-up scene early on. It's where we really see the effect Claire has on Richard ... Ashley. They're having a weekend in the country. With her old college friends. I got the idea from these get-togethers of yours. I want them to be in love. But then I guess they can't be if she's such a cow.

Simian Anyway, if they were in love, there wouldn't be any reason for Ashley to want Claire modifed. This young woman should be a heartbreaker. Affairs all over the place. She won't settle until she's ready. And then she'll have a whole set of reasons for doing so. She needs to regard her difficulties with Richard ... Ashley ... with absolutely no sympathy at all.

Richard So you don't think there's any room for her to be sympathetic — so the reader can make an emotional investment in her.

Simian Why? She's only in the story so she can hurt Richard ... er, Ashley. That's the truth.

Richard (*suddenly very dark*) If Emma carried on like that, I'd be tempted to kill her myself.

Tony (*shocked*) Would you? Hmm. Well, you'd better keep a check on yourself, Richard. (*A little bitterly*) I was just thinking how much your character Claire actually reminds me of Emma ... (*He takes a big gulp of whisky*)

Richard What makes you say that?

Tony (*awkwardly*) Nothing.

Simian I'm afraid there's some history there, Richard. (*He briskly changes the subject*) Well, your story's getting better. More edge. Maybe if he's mad enough, then he'd rather beat Claire's brains out than let her become independent of him.

Richard I can identify with that. I mean, sometimes, when you're really in love, well — you get sort of unbalanced, don't you?

Simian You heard him, Tony. We're both witnesses to his confession, right?

Tony So, do you believe in all that voodoo stuff?

Richard No. I don't really believe in anything beyond what I can see or hear.

Tony Fancy that. Still, it makes sense. I suppose you need clinical detachment, so you can marshal your tricks properly. No use frightening yourself.

Richard Oh, I've done that a few times. Quite nice when it happens.

Tony Still, good not to have to worry about whether or not evil really exists.

Richard There is evil all right. (*He pauses*) It's behind the screen when people sit on the edge of their sofas, craning forward, staring gormlessly. It's in the boozy crap puffed-up morons spout down the pub. The lies, the ignorance, the assumptions that underpin ... cruelty. Violence. All the million crimes we take for granted. (*He imitates a foul-mouthed mother*) "Here, Wayne, you little sod!" The deceptions of those who say they love us.

Tony (*who has drunk quite a bit by now*) Right. Yes. Very good. (*He pauses*) Look, I tell you what. I've got a bit of a yarn, Richard. Don't know, might be useful to you. It's not spooky. Well, it is. But it's not to do with ghosts and the like. It's true. I mean it's about truth.

Simian Big subject, Tony.

Tony Don't tease me, Simian. (*He sets himself up, ready to spin the yarn*) OK. First term at university. Long before I got involved with Simian. I joined an outdoor pursuits club. There was this guy, Philip ... Philip Something. Oh, what was it? Nope. Gone. Anyway, Philip something-or-other.

Simian Get on with it, Tony.

Tony He attached himself to our group. Nobody felt particularly comfortable with him. One of those stray dog types, so we just tolerated him. Made him buy plenty of rounds — as a penance for being boring. So, first term early November we all bugger off to a caving cottage in Yorkshire. It's the first day, and people are arriving in dribs and drabs. We're meeting in the village pub. Jack and I get there early, and this bloke Philip turns up. So we all walk up to the cottage. About two miles. Totally isolated place. Can't even get a car up there. We sort things out a bit, then decide to walk back down to the pub and wait for the others. Only Philip decides he's not coming. Why? (*He shrugs his shoulders*) Won't say. Just insists on staying by himself.

Anyway, a couple of hours later, there's half a dozen of us assembled in the pub. Jeremy's completely knackered. Asks if someone will walk up with him so he can get some kip. I volunteer, and we set off. The light is starting to go. Bright enough on the hills, but very murky in the dips and hollows. Mist coming up off the streams. A few early stars even. So we come over the brow of the hill, and there's the cottage in the deep shadows below. Straight away, I know there's something really badly wrong. No lights. Why's Philip sitting down there in the dark? We walk forward and downhill. It's like someone's turning the lights down. Like Orpheus descending. About a hundred yards off, and it's obvious every window — upstairs and down — has been smashed in. Bloody Hell! So. The front door is ajar. And it's pitch dark inside. I tell Jeremy to stay where he is, and if anything nasty happens, he's to run for help. Agreed. Now, I'm not going in through that door. Instead, I go round the side and climb in through the kitchen window. Broken glass everywhere. My eyes get used to the dark. The sink unit has been pulled off the wall. There's a car battery smashed across the floor. I move through the hallway. Just the crunch of glass, and my heart pounding in my ears. There's an orange glow from the living room. The door's half open and I can see about a third of it. There are great horizontal slashes of blood up the walls — like in a horror movie. There had been stuffed animals in glass cases, hanging on the walls. But they'd been ripped apart and strewn about. So I gently push at the door. It swings open, and there's Philip. He's sitting in the middle of the floor. He's got no trousers on, and he's shit himself. He stares at me. Still got his specs on. Odd considering. His hands are cut to ribbons, and he's holding up this long dagger of window glass. (*He stops, suspended in the memory of it*)

Richard What happened to him?

Tony (*after a pause*) Sorry. Not up to your standard, I'm sure.

Richard You can't just stop. What happened to him?

Tony Anyway, we got it sorted. I sat with him for eighteen hours while he came down. Then we took him to a doctor. Made up some story. Spent the rest of the week re-glazing the house. Of course this Philip bloke was never really right. He'd dropped out of college by Christmas. To be honest, everyone was pleased to see the back of him. Couldn't abide the way he loomed about in the shadows. Not speaking. (*He pauses*) So, any use to you, Richard?

Richard I don't know. Is it really true?

Tony Absolutely.

Simian It has the ring of truth. Maybe that means it's not got the edge Richard likes.

Richard Have you read my stuff, then?

Tony (*butting in*) Another drink, anyone? Hey! Look at the time. It's a quarter to ten. The toast. It's come and gone without us. End of an era.

Simian (*genuinely upset*) Damn!

Richard I saw the time. But I thought you'd want to wait for Emma.

Simian (*looking venomously toward Richard*) The rituals one invents give
a shape to things. Give a contour to the years. Oh, well. I suppose we'd
better get on with preparing for supper. I'm sure Emma will be famished
when she does get here.

Richard Can I go up and sort myself out?

Simian Yes. Sure. You're at the top, right at the end of the corridor.

Richard takes his bag from the hallway and exits upstairs

Tony Seems a nice chap. What about Emma? Time's getting on. Poor
driving conditions, after all.

Simian Well, we'll give her another hour, then I'll call the police. Help
yourself to another drink. I'll be in the kitchen. (*He turns to go, then turns
back*) Don't mention the possibility of an accident to Richard. I'm sure
there's nothing to worry about. Yes. I'm sure.

Simian exits into the kitchen

Richard (*calling from upstairs*) Tony!

Tony (*moving into the hallway*) Yep?

Richard (*off*) I meant to ask. How formal is the meal?

Tony Oh, Simian would like it to be black tie. But we talked him out of it
last year.

Richard (*off*) That's a relief.

Tony I'm not going to bother changing. Think I'll phone Gerald's family.
Give them my best.

Richard (*off*) Terrible thing. Down in a minute.

*Tony goes to the telephone, pauses for a moment, then lifts the receiver and
dials*

Tony (*into the phone*) Hallo. Could I speak to Dorothy, please? ... Dorothy?
Hallo. It's Tony. How are you? ... Yes, I'm at Simian's. I was terribly sorry
to hear about Gerald. Simian told me. ... What do you mean? ... OK, yes.
I'll let you get back to them. Maybe we should try and meet sometime. ...
Bye, then. (*He puts the phone down and stands still, looking worried*)

Simian enters suddenly

Simian By the way ——

Tony (*surprised by Simian's sudden entrance*) Oh!

Simian Sorry. Who were you talking to?

Tony I wanted to say how sorry I was about Gerald's death.

Simian Did you speak to Dorothy?

Tony Yes, I did.

Simian Did you mention Richard?

Tony No. Why would I? (*He pauses*) She said Gerald was here just before he killed himself. Came to spend the weekend, then went home and did it. Why didn't you tell me?

Simian You know I was very proud of Gerald. I just didn't want to talk about it — to go over it all again.

Tony Of course. Sorry.

Simian I was going to say, I really do want to talk to you about your future. That job on the *Caledonian Times*. You could do a lot better.

Tony Look, Simian ——

Simian All right! Just listen, will you? You know I thought you were better suited to medicine, but if it's going to be newspapers, then I think you should aim higher. I've got some useful contacts. I'm not going to let you leave here without a promise that you'll at least let me try and get you into the newsroom of one of the Sunday heavies.

Tony Simian, I don't know.

Simian You would have to move back to London. Emma's always saying how much she misses you. It would be good for you both, I'm sure.

Tony True. Mind you, she's so busy these days. And of course she's got Richard.

Simian Emma misses your down-to-earth personality. She says you're very "rooted". I know for a fact she's fed up with the theatre scene. And as for Richard ... Well, I wouldn't put too much store by all that.

Tony Fine. Well ... Let me have a think.

Simian Look, I mean what I say. You're not leaving here without making that promise.

Tony All right then.

Simian Excellent. (*He moves to exit to the kitchen again, then turns back as if struck by an idea*) I know! I'll make sure you can't pull out of this one.

Tony Come off it, Simian.

Simian No, Tony. I'm serious. We'll have a contract.

Tony So what would I forfeit, then?

Simian I don't know. I'll have to think about that. Your eternal soul, perhaps.

Tony and Simian both laugh

The actors freeze and the lights cross-fade to an eerie blue wash

SCENE 2

The hallway is in darkness. The living-room is illuminated by the Christmas tree, table lamp and firelight

Simian and Tony are seated on the sofa. Tony is asleep, obviously drunk

As the scene begins, Simian fills Tony's glass from a fresh bottle of whisky. He then forces the whisky down Tony's throat. Tony drifts back into stupor

Emma and Richard enter the room without noise. Emma wears an expensive joke shop hag mask. She looms over Tony

Drunken Tony becomes conscious of Emma, and jumps

Tony Ahh!
Emma (*removing the mask*) Sorry, Tony. Couldn't resist it.
Tony Bloody horrible, Emma. Where'd it come from?
Emma Party I was at earlier on. Quite life-like, don't you think so, Simian?
Simian Mmm. I've seen better.
Emma Sorry about the wait. I had to get changed.
Simian Don't worry, you're always worth waiting for, Emma. But I'm sorry to say Tony's pretty much out for the count. Richard. Sorry to be a pain. D'you think you could get him up to his room while I make up a plate of supper for Emma?
Richard Of course.

Richard helps the bleary-eyed Tony to his feet

Come on, Tony. Let's get you upstairs.

They head for the stairs

Tony Heavens! Yes. Sorry, Emma. You're here! Hurray! (*He staggers*) Sorry. It's your fault. Waiting for you to arrive, couldn't help myself. That fatal bottle too far. Never mind. We'll talk in the morning, right? (*He pauses*) God, Emma. You're bloody gorgeous! (*He attempts to kiss Emma*)
Emma (*avoiding Tony's attempt*) 'Night Tony. See you in the morning.
Richard Back soon.

Richard and Tony exit

Emma and Simian are alone. Simian returns to the drinks cabinet and stashes the new bottle inside at the back

Simian He's right. You look wonderful, Emma.
Emma Did you get what you needed from Tony?
Simian A promise of sorts.
Emma And what about Richard?
Simian All over bar the shouting.
Emma So he hasn't —
Simian He's close. (*He pauses*) Come here, Emma.
Emma Simian —
Simian Please come over here, Emma.
Emma It would be very nice if we had a chance to talk, Simian.
Simian What about, Emma?
Emma Well, this partnership. It's getting a little —
Simian Cloying? Wearing?
Emma I wasn't going to say that.
Simian Because if you were feeling worn out with it, then maybe we'd better look at bringing the agreement to a conclusion.
Emma I wasn't meaning that.
Simian As you know, we have drawn things out well beyond what either of us could have expected. Sometimes it's a relief to get things over with. When they're in decline.
Emma I didn't mean —
Simian Thing is, I'm not fed up with you.
Emma Good.
Simian And actually, if I were in your shoes, I'd breathe a sigh of relief over that. Of course these things are precarious. A word out of place, or a request denied —
Emma Please don't bully me, Simian.
Simian Bully you? I assure you, Emma. If I was wanting to bully you, you'd know it. Now, I'd like you to come here.

Richard enters from upstairs

Richard Poor old Tony! He seems very off-colour.
Simian Maybe he's picked up some sort of bug.

Emma perches on the L end of the sofa

Richard I was wondering if we should call the doctor out.
Simian No. I'm sure he'll be fine. Anyway I don't rate our chances of getting a physician on New Year's Eve in this weather, do you? (*He sits in the armchair*)

Richard Guess not. (*He refills his glass — not from the bottle Simian has just handled. There is a pause*) Can I get another drink for anyone?

Emma No.

Simian No thanks.

Richard (*sitting between Emma and Simian*) Emma. You are looking gorgeous.

Emma That makes it a hat trick.

Richard What?

Emma Everyone is being very nice this evening. But you know you wouldn't have recognized me before Simian came along.

Richard With all due respect to Simian, he couldn't have helped if nature hadn't taken a hand first.

Emma You're making me blush. (*She pauses*) Do you remember an old episode of *Star Trek*, where some benign aliens put the captain together with this sultry woman, only they'd done something to his mind, and he couldn't see her as she really was. The aliens had put her face back together after a crash. But they'd never seen a human, and didn't know which bits went where. (*Pause*) The real-life doctors called it commando surgery, back in the seventies. (*Pause*) When I was small. (*Pause*) So, I was an absolute wallflower when I arrived at Cambridge. Simian sorted me out. Changed my life. (*She indicates the left side of her face*) All gone.

Richard Why didn't you tell me?

Emma As I said. Simian took care of it.

Richard So, how did you manage that, Simian?

Emma Simian has all kinds of friends. Everywhere.

Simian Called in a debt or two.

Richard That's why she's so loyal to you.

Emma But there's a price. What I didn't realize beforehand, is that looking good has a great deal in common with being — the opposite. When you're ashamed of how you look ... Frightened. You scurry about like a little creature. Hiding your face. Combing your hair across. Wear a hat, or a hood, when the weather's perfectly OK. Read a magazine upright like a spy. Hide by holding your temple as though deep in thought. Anything to avoid stalling people's conversation, then hear them start up again, audibly relieved that they, and theirs, are not like you. But, when you're pretty, you hide all over again. When you were misshapen, theirs was a gruesome fascination. Now it's malevolence. When you're pretty people want to hurt you. Men think the presence of beauty gives them rights. That you look like you do for their sakes. And they are entitled to do what they want with you. They stare at your mouth. Not your eyes. At your breasts, your legs, your backside. You can have a first from Cambridge but really you're only a torso to be gawped at. What I don't understand is how it works out that, almost the moment he's got you, a man sets about pulling you apart.

Squeezing the life out. Maiming. Diluting you. Laying waste to everything he found desirable. Why do that? Why reduce you in that way? Make you into a creature he can despise. I suppose, when he says he loves you, he really means that he hates you. He doesn't want to "look after" you at all. He really wants to pillage and despoil. He wants to fuck you, and to punch you — both at the same time.

Richard Look, I really don't get this.

Simian I'll take you through it.

Richard Through what?

Simian It strikes me you've done surprisingly well, Richard.

Richard Oh, I don't know.

Simian No false modesty, now. After all, you did very well considering how hard your bloody parents tried to mess you up.

Richard I can say that. You can't.

Simian They're your words, not mine.

Richard I didn't ... When ... ?

Simian I made it my job to take in people on the margins. Those who had to work really hard, and could so easily be overlooked. It's impressive to see you've made such a success of yourself without the benefit of a — Svengali.

Richard Thanks, Simian.

Simian I think it's time you joined the others.

Richard What others?

Simian Those who attend our annual gathering.

Richard But I thought we were it.

Simian In here, yes. But there are many more visitors. Just out of view. You see them sometimes. A movement on the edge of your vision. And when you look around. Search about for them. They're not there! Between you and me, it's just as well. If you got a good look at them, you'd wish you hadn't. (*Pause*) Listen.

Richard What?

Emma Listen!

The three of them are still

We hear distant music, as if an old waltz is playing in an ancient ballroom

Richard Where's that coming from?

Simian If you go out through the kitchen, beyond the tack room, you come to the original part of the house. What you see around you here: this is all the nineteenth-century extension. The original part of the house is much older. I mean really old. You have to go down a steep flight of steps. That's where everybody meets. Down there.

The atmosphere lightens

Richard (*realizing it has all been a ruse*) So, there is a party after all. Ah! I see. A masquerade — a charade sort of thing. New Year's Night.

Simian That's right. A lot of old friends. But it doesn't usually get going until after midnight, and we thought we'd make it a surprise for you. I think you'll be thrilled. You can join them now. And I hope you'll share this evening with us again, time after time after time. You're very welcome here, Richard.

Richard Thank you very much, Simian. I'll confess I was dreading tonight. I don't like all that Oxbridge stuff. But I am pleased to have met you after all, Simian.

Simian This isn't actually the first time we've met.

Richard Isn't it? Well in that case I'm really sorry, but I don't remember. Oh, look, before things get going: can I use your phone to find out about my car?

Emma What happened just before your accident? The thought of Emma — me — made you angry. "Just a twitch of the steering wheel. Then she'd be sorry." You told me that Tony was held up by a fatal crash on the A1.

Richard (*after a pause*) Ah, spooky stories. Very good. My stock-in-trade. Hang on. Before we get any further into it, can I phone the garage?

Simian (*firmly*) No.

Richard (*equally firmly*) Yes.

Simian (*placing his hand on the telephone*)What garage?

Emma You do know him.

Richard Do I?

Simian "Snow is falling. It swirls in illuminated cones of sodium yellow — under each street light. He turns down an alleyway. His shoes mark the virgin snow. Behind him, another pair of shoes make a second, silent trail."

Emma They're waiting for you. Just past the kitchen. Head for the tack room, Richard. Then you'll hear them.

Richard All right. (*He laughs out loud*) I'll go and look. It's a brilliant performance. I won't forgive you, Emma, if you've got some actor friend of yours dressed up as Beelzebub, all set to jump out on me. (*He moves as if to to exit into the kitchen*) Hang on. OK, suppose I'm already dead, and you're Mephistopheles. Big question. Why not project me straight from the car wreck to the tar pit? What's this evening been about?

Simian It has to hurt. You have to be brought slowly to the knowledge of what you've done. Most of all, you have to see the barren nature of the treasures that drew you in. Your ambition and ——

Richard Emma. All right. Fine. Where's the fiery furnace? What about Tony? Is he having a go?

Simian Sooner or later. Everyone has to do it. Nobody goes with you, though. You have to do it on your own.

Richard (*entering into the spirit of the charade*) Supposing the devil does get me, how will you explain my disappearance?

Emma The police have already extricated your body from that crashed car.

Richard Ah, ha! But Tony knows I was here after the crash.

Simian Tony has contracted a nasty gastric infection which will keep him upstairs, delirious, for roughly two days. And when he surfaces, I'll tell him he arrived with a fever, and never actually saw you. Just dreamed you.

Emma There's poetry in that. It's true, in a way.

Simian moves about collecting glasses and putting away bottles during the following

Simian He will have a vague recollection that we spoke about you. That something was very wrong in your relationship with Emma. That you were terribly possessive. It's a short step to suicide.

Richard But Emma and I love each other. We're not like my characters.

Simian Emma and I have become very close —— (*He switches off the Christmas tree lights, then sits on the sofa beside Emma*)

Emma Familiar, one might say.

Richard Yeah, yeah. (*He applauds the others*) Well done. Won't you come with me, Emma? Introduce me to people.

Emma No. You're big enough to look after yourself. Besides, it's a journey we all have to make alone. No-one's allowed to go with you. I'll be along. In time.

Richard Very good, both of you. Creepy. OK, I'll go and see what you've set up for us. Back soon.

Richard exits

Emma and Simian sit quite still, next to one another

Simian Sit up, please.

There is a pause. Emma sits up

I should think Richard's being sick about now. And pissing himself.

Emma Will I be sick? And ——

Simian (*looking hard at Emma*) Probably. But you don't need to worry about that yet. You're still young. And will remain so for a long time to come.

The radio comes on, increasing in volume; we hear the hiss of static and sounds of distant lands. The stage is flooded with a lurid ethereal light. The radio becomes unbearably loud, then suddenly cuts out, accompanied by a simultaneous Black-out

FAST CURTAIN

FURNITURE AND PROPERTY LIST

SCENE 1

Set:　LIVING-ROOM/KITCHEN
Sideboard. *In it*: bottle of whisky, glasses
Kitchen range. *On it*: pans and utensils — including two wooden
　　spoons — for cooking meat and vegetables, kettle. *By it*: poker
Comfortable upright chair
Kitchen table. *On it*: chess game set up for **Father** and **Herbert**
Chairs
On mantelpiece: photograph of Steven in uniform, figure of Madonna,
　　chess set
Low table. *On it*: large valve radio

SCULLERY
On bracket: keys

Personal:　**Morris**: monkey's paw
Father: coins

SCENE 2

Set:　LIVING-ROOM/KITCHEN
Glass of whisky for **Father**

SCULLERY
Dirty dishes
Tea towel

Re-set:　Cooking pans, utensils and glasses to sink in scullery
Chess pieces back into box

SCENE 3

Set:　LIVING-ROOM/KITCHEN
Herbert's coat on peg
Nearly-finished breakfast for **Herbert**

Re-set: Paw on table

Strike: Dishes, pans, utensils, glasses from scullery
                 Whisky glass

Off stage: Brown envelope containing bill (**Father**)

SCENE 4

Set: LIVING-ROOM/KITCHEN
                 Plate of sandwiches for **Mother**

SCENE 5

Set: LIVING-ROOM/KITCHEN
                 Oil lamp on table

Re-set: Paw on bracket in scullery

THE DARK

SCENE 1

On stage: Cocktail cabinet. *On it*: selection of malt whiskies, large valve radio.
                     In it: glasses
                 Tastefully decorated Christmas tree
                 French period style armchair
                 Expensive sofa
                 Elegant coffee table. *On it*: ashtray and table lighter
                 Small occasional table. *On it*: telephone, address book, table lamp
                 On mantelpiece: clock, cigar box
                 In hallway, out of sight: **Richard**'s bag

Personal: **Richard**: handkerchief

SCENE 2

Off stage: Joke shop hag mask (**Emma**)

LIGHTING PLOT

Practical fittings required: glow from range, light from radio dial
Interior. The same throughout

SCENE 1

To open: General interior lighting with glow from range and dial on radio lit up

| *Cue* 1 | **Mother** turns the radio off | (Page 1) |
| | *Cut radio light* | |

| *Cue* 2 | **Morris**: "Famished, Jean." | (Page 6) |
| | *Dim lights; bring up radio light* | |

SCENE 2

To open: General interior lighting with glow from range and radio light

| *Cue* 3 | Music fades | (Page 7) |
| | *Cut radio light* | |

| *Cue* 4 | **Herbert** brushes the paw | (Page 9) |
| | *Dim lights; bring up radio light* | |

SCENE 3

To open: General interior lighting; bright morning lighting on exterior backing; radio light

| *Cue* 5 | Music fades | (Page 9) |
| | *Cut radio light* | |

| *Cue* 6 | **Mother** turns the radio on | (Page 10) |
| | *Bring up radio light* | |

| *Cue* 7 | **Father** makes up the fire | (Page 10) |
| | *Dim lights* | |

SCENE 4

To open: General interior lighting; evening lighting on exterior backing

| *Cue* 8 | **Father** and the **Man** exit | (Page 13) |
| | *Dim lights; bring up radio light* | |

SCENE 5

To open: General interior lighting; moonlight on exterior backing; practical oil lamp on with covering spot

No cues

THE DARK

Practical fittings required: fireglow in grate; table lamp; light from radio dial; Christmas tree lights
Interior. The same throughout

SCENE 1

To open: All practicals on

| *Cue* 1 | **Simian** switches the room lights on | (Page 20) |
| | *Bring up general interior lighting* | |

| *Cue* 2 | **Simian** switches on the hall light | (Page 20) |
| | *Bring up light in hallway* | |

| *Cue* 3 | **Simian** switches the radio off | (Page 21) |
| | *Cut radio dial light* | |

| *Cue* 4 | The actors freeze | (Page 33) |
| | *Cross-fade to eerie blue wash* | |

SCENE 2

To open: Christmas tree, fireglow and table lamp

| *Cue* 5 | **Simian** switches off the Christmas tree lights | (Page 39) |
| | *Cut Christmas tree lights* | |

| *Cue* 6 | **Simian**: " ... for a long time to come." | (Page 39) |
| | *Radio light on; lurid ethereal light over stage* | |

| *Cue* 7 | Radio becomes unbearably loud | (Page 39) |
| | *Black-out* | |

EFFECTS PLOT

THE MONKEY'S PAW

Cue 1	When play begins *Rain and occasional gusts of wind; Forties dance hit* *from radio*	(Page 1)
Cue 2	**Mother** turns off the radio *Snap off radio sound*	(Page 1)
Cue 3	**Mother** opens the front door *Increase volume of rain and wind sounds*	(Page 1)
Cue 4	**Mother** closes the front door *Decrease volume of rain and wind sounds*	(Page 1)
Cue 5	**Father** opens the front door *Increase volume of rain and wind sounds*	(Page 2)
Cue 6	**Father** closes the front door *Decrease volume of rain and wind sounds*	(Page 2)
Cue 7	The lights dim; radio dial lights up *Music; a Forties dance hit*	(Page 6)
Cue 8	As SCENE 2 begins *Fade music; rain effect*	(Page 7)
Cue 9	They all settle at the table *Wind rises; door bangs upstairs*	(Page 8)
Cue 10	Lights dim; radio light comes on *Music; Frank Sinatra's "Blue Skies"*	(Page 9)
Cue 11	When SCENE 3 begins *Fade music*	(Page 9)
Cue 12	**Mother** switches the radio on *Short wave static, undulating whine*	(Page 10)
Cue 13	Lights dim *Bring up volume of radio sound; fade to silence when ready*	(Page 10)

Cue 15   Lights dim; radio light comes on   (Page 13)
             Radio; distant exotic languages and static

Cue 16   When SCENE 5 begins   (Page 13)
             Fade radio to silence

Cue 18   **Mother** and **Father** sit still and united   (Page 15)
             Quiet scratching at door; pause; more scratching

Cue 19   **Father**: "I saw it in the yard last night."   (Page 15)
             Huge knock resounds through house

Cue 20   **Mother**: "Herbert. It's me."   (Page 15)
             Knock at front door; then continuous knocking
             until Cue 21

Cue 21   **Father** slowly opens his palm   (Page 16)
             Stop knocking

Cue 22   **Mother** hauls open the door   (Page 16)
             Sound of cold breeze

Cue 23   **Mother** closes the door   (Page 16)
             Fade breeze sound

Cue 24   **Mother** begins climbing the stairs   (Page 16)
             Knock from back door

Cue 25   **Father**: "It does things a crooked way,"   (Page 16)
             Heavy, urgent knocking; continuous to end of scene

Cue 26   **Father**: "God in Heaven, help us please."   (Page 16)
             Bring in echo effect on knocking; increase volume
             to fill auditorium

THE DARK

Cue 1   As play begins   (Page 19)
             Gale blowing outside; continues quietly throughout play.
             Radio plays closing phrases of "Iolanthe", then
             Radio Announcer*'s voice, dialogue pp. 19-20*

Cue 2   **Radio Announcer**: *"The Monkey's Paw."*   (Page 19)
             Robust knock at front door

Cue 3   **Simian** puts his jacket on   (Page 19)
             Loud rapping at the door

Cue 4	**Simian** tidies a cushion *Another knock*	(Page 20)
Cue 5	**Simian** turns the radio off *Cut radio sound*	(Page 21)
Cue 6	**Richard**: "Where the fuck ... Sorry." *Loud knock at the door*	(Page 23)
Cue 7	**Emma**: "Listen." They are still *Distant music; old waltz*	(Page 37)
Cue 8	**Simian**: "... for a long time to come." *Radio on; increase volume until unbearably loud then cut*	(Page 39)